The Silent Jesus

Learning from Our Lord's Life of Prayer

Mike Wallbridge

R. Thomas Ashbrook

RESOURCE *Publications* · Eugene, Oregon

THE SILENT JESUS
Learning from Our Lord's Life of Prayer

Resource Publications
An Imprint of Wipf and Stock Publishers
199 W. 8th Ave., Suite 3
Eugene, OR 97401

www.wipfandstock.com

PAPERBACK ISBN: 978-1-6667-0132-6
HARDCOVER ISBN: 978-1-6667-0133-3
EBOOK ISBN: 978-1-6667-0134-0

07/01/21

Contents

Foreword

Meeting you here, just inside the front cover of Mike Wallbridge's book about Jesus, tells me something exciting about you. We're each here because we want to know Jesus more deeply and to serve him with more passion and faithfulness. We want more; we're "hungry and thirsty." Maybe, like me, you also long for more for the Church. Often connected with our personal stuck feelings, we find that we're also concerned with the institutional church, unsure whether the Church is transforming our world into the Kingdom of God or the world is forming the Church into *its* image.

Having served as a parish pastor for some decades, and now as a spiritual formation missionary, I have become very familiar with the hungry and thirsty realm. Jesus says that we are blessed when we find ourselves hungry and thirsty for righteousness and for deep intimacy with God in Christ. Yet, so many of us feel guilty when we find ourselves dissatisfied. But we are seeing Christians all over the world abandoning the false idea that we should feel satisfied with the status quo of our own faith. They're trading in their false guilt to embrace a new zeal to know our Lord more deeply, standing boldly in the Apostle Paul's passion expressed in Philippians 3:10: "To want to know Christ and the power of his resurrection and the fellowship of sharing in his sufferings." You're blessed if you are hungry and thirsty for more of your Lord and blessed to be pursuing your longing within these pages.

Considering our longing, however, aren't you curious about launching into a book with the title, "The Silent Jesus?" For most of us, "silent" represents the last thing we want! We long for a Jesus we can see and hear, a Jesus who teaches and directs us and guides us into the places where miracles happen, and lives are changed!

Maybe to explain what he means by silence, Mike will take us back through time into the years that Jesus ministered physically in what we now call the Mideast, to intersect the amazing events of miracles, private conversations with the disciples, and confrontations with the religious leaders? What if we could become present at Jesus' baptism, the feeding of the five thousand, gaze on Jesus on the mount of transfiguration, eavesdrop on his prayers in the Garden of Gethsemane, watch the agony of the crucifixion, and witness his glorious resurrection?

Imagine, after such an experience, meeting together, maybe on the Mount of Olives or by the Sea of Tiberias, to debrief our experiences. Once we'd compiled all that we'd learned, our focus would soon turn to the times to which we are about to return. How might our lives change? How might our ministries become transformed by what we have learned? Imagine sharing our experiences and teaching our amazing insights! We could easily envision a Church transformed and cultures shining with new love and compassion!

If my imaginary story sounds like what you want to find in the following pages, I would advise you to stop right here; just put the book down.

You see, if we think about it, our imaginary pilgrimage back through time and space sounds a lot like what we learned in Sunday school or Bible college or seminary. It's not unlike most sermons we have heard or even given—filled with information. What we've learned has certainly been useful in our spiritual growth and in our ability to live as disciples of Jesus. Yet we've rendezvoused inside the front cover of this little book because we've realized we need more than information—much more!

Fortunately, however, I think you'll soon agree that we're meeting in the right place. Instead of simply teaching us new truths and strategies for spiritual growth, Mike opens his life to us. How refreshing to be invited beyond information into the story of one man's encounter with God in the midst of spiritual hunger and thirst. The Silent Jesus paints a picture of someplace that Bible college or seminary or our imaginary journey can't take us. Mike points us to a land far deeper than just the experiences and teachings of Scripture; he shows us a pathway into the heart of God where we can come to know him more deeply and intimately than we might imagine possible. Mike shows us how to let our Good Shepherd guide us into the kind of relationship he has with the Trinity—one that he demonstrated to his disciples—a relationship called Silence. Through Mike's story of his own discoveries in prayer, you'll also glimpse a new level of discipleship marked with the fruit of one who simply knows Jesus.

Now that we've become clear about what our hearts long for, let's turn the page and meet my brother, Mike. He and I first met about fifteen years ago when he served as the librarian in an obscure castle in Austria. I had been writing and teaching about the spiritual journey based on historical mystics such as Teresa of Avila and John of the Cross. In Mike, however, I soon realized that I had been befriended by a modern mystic whose life uniquely embodies the movements of the Holy Spirit described in Scripture and in men and women through the ages who follow Jesus into the heart of God. You'll find that Mike won't ask you to try to emulate his experience but to simply let the Holy Spirit speak to you, simultaneously satisfying your hunger and thirst and then enflaming your desire even more. Thank you, Mike, for your humble obedience in writing *The Silent Jesus*.

R. Thomas Ashbrook

Author of *Mansions of the Heart, Presence,* and *Contagious Fire,* Dr. Ashbrook holds a DMin degree in Spiritual Formation from Portland Seminary. Now a spiritual formation consultant, Tom teaches on the subject and provides spiritual direction and spiritual formation coaching to Christian leaders.

Preface

IN MY LATE TWENTIES, I developed a passion for walking the mountains of the English Lake District near where I lived, spending my holidays on the higher summits of North Wales and Scotland. Not yet a believer, I sought some sense of "spirituality" and transcendence in the challenge and adrenaline of a climb. The higher the mountain, the more difficult the route, the greater the accompanying "high." In time, my eyes wandered to the trekking paths and more accessible peaks of the Himalayas, the arena of my climbing heroes. I had walked mainly alone, enjoying the solitude and the stillness, but these I knew would require a guide familiar with the territory and the routes.

The spiritual life of the Christian follows similar geography, a pilgrimage over mountains and through valleys we undertake alone, perhaps more often among friends on similar journeys. In place of a map and compass, a pastor and the Bible help keep us on track. But the deeper we go into the spiritual life into an intimate relationship with God, and the higher we set our heights, the more we need an experienced guide familiar with the more challenging pathways and terrain.

I never did get to the Himalayas. God came into my life, and my priorities changed overnight. I will share my story later, but, ironically, it began high in those Himalayas, spiritually speaking. A powerful Damascus Road-type conversion led to two years in which God met me in a series of extraordinary encounters. Then they stopped . . . never to return, leaving a hunger in me to walk again in those high places of intimacy, of deep communion with God. I have spent the last twenty-five years studying the territory and the pathways—in my prayer life, at theological college, and with a spiritual director.

I have not yet attained the Himalayan heights where my story began. Few of us ever do, and it is by God's grace alone, anyway. But their lowly foothills, in which I wander daily, are still a constant delight and source of blessing and fruit. My relationship with God deepens, and I live increasingly like Jesus in peace and tranquility. It is along those pathways I would like to lead you.

Why? Because I believe most of us do not follow Jesus in the most fundamental of ways he would wish us to. Deep down, our Christian walk is far less dictated by what we learn of Jesus in the Gospels than by identities determined for us by society. And that is not only disappointing, but it prevents us from living out the fullness of a relationship with Jesus, with God.

Before we begin, let me make one thing clear: this book is not intended for people like me, with my unusual spiritual background, but for *all* Christians desiring a deeper relationship with God, although it may appeal more to older believers, in age and faith. God longs for all his children to journey along this path, following Jesus' life of prayer deeper into communion and intimacy with the Father. The way is one of silence, hence the title of this book. This is not the negative silence of an absent God, an idea influenced by some impressions we have from events in Old Testament history, but a silence that welcomes and embraces God's presence.

I have laid this book out as follows. In an introduction, I want to reveal to you a Jesus you may never have considered, or perhaps only in passing. In chapter 1, I examine Scriptures concerning his prayer life, in particular the notion of his silence before God. In chapter 2, I look at the nature of such silent prayer, and in chapter 3, I will confirm my findings in the context of the Old Testament and Christian history. In chapter 4, I want to examine what the word "relationship" means, especially as regards our relationship with God, and chapter 5 places silent prayer within two comprehensive models of prayer. In chapter 6, I devote my attention to ministry and its relationship with prayer, and in chapter 7, I want to guide you into the practice of silent prayer itself. In chapter 8, I will talk about the fruit of such prayer, and in chapter 9 I will suggest an alternative to silent prayer for those whose lives are too busy to make room for it. In chapter 10, I will share with you something of my story and follow that with conclusions in chapter 11.

Acknowledgments

IN WRITING THIS BOOK, I am deeply indebted to James Houston and Eugene Peterson, professors of spiritual theology at Regent College, Vancouver, during the blessed years I studied there. Between them, they introduced me to new and rich vistas of understanding about prayer and relationship with God, and I left Regent College a changed person. Another professor to whom I'm grateful, Charles Ringma, guided me through my final comprehensive paper, a labor of love that provided me with the seed for this book.

Though God initially put the book on my heart, I would like to thank my friend, Murray Watts, for encouraging me and giving me the confidence to write it. Both he and my mentor friend, Tom Ashbrook, gave me good advice and criticism on my first draft. Tom was kind enough to write a foreword for me too. Friends Norm Heinrichs-Gale, Larry Lighty, Karin Durfey, and Andy Fraser also provided encouragement and helpful input and deserve my thanks along with those who have consented to endorse the book.

My thanks go to Bill Reimer at Regent College Publishing for his help with permissions and for introducing Wipf and Stock to me as a potential publisher. I must also mention Matthew Wimer and everyone at Wipf and Stock for steering me through the complex publishing process and for copyeditor Christy Callahan for turning my raw and British writing into a polished manuscript for an American audience.

Though I cannot begin to list them all, I would like to say thank you too to all those who have regularly prayed for my writing and health over the years. Without your faithful support, this book would never have been started.

Last, but not least, I must thank my wonderful wife, Livia, for her encouragement and support of this book and her willingness to prayerfully read and comment on everything I put in front of her . . . and my heavenly Father for his inspiration and guidance, his love and strength. Thank you, Father!

Introduction

We Christians have many ways to describe ourselves, among them "believers" or "disciples" or "followers of Jesus," who is our Lord but also our role model. He told the disciples, "Whoever believes in me will do the works I have been doing, and they will do even greater things than these" (John 14:12). But, sadly, few of us follow Jesus when it comes to his life of prayer. Few of us are aware of it, let alone understand it.

When we read the Gospels to understand Jesus and his life, our focus usually is on what he said and what he did (i.e., his ministry). These four books are the source of all Jesus' teachings, including the parables, and also provide a picture of his healing and deliverance ministry. But they portray another side to Jesus, although one not made explicit and therefore easy to overlook. Because of my unusual story and theological study, my interest is less in what he said and did, important though they are, than in the way he *was*—and the way he related to the Father. The latter, his personal prayer life, is vital to understand, I believe, if we are to follow him as closely as he desires and to find the key to the way he lived and ministered.

But first, let's take a look at how Jesus *was*. Reading the Gospels as story, we see a Jesus who, for most of the time, walked through life in unhurried peace and calmness.[1] In fact, he was so unrushed that, to our knowledge, at least two people died because he would not allow himself to be dictated to by circumstances. They were, of course, Jairus' daughter and Lazarus. Fortunately, the stories did not end there, and God received greater

---

1. With the exception of Gethsemane as his time grew closer, when he sweated blood (Luke 22:44).

glory through Jesus raising them from the dead. But in a busy world full of need, poverty, and sickness, Jesus walked through first-century Israel with apparent ease, living in the moment in the presence and love of the Father, compassionate but determined to do "what he sees his Father doing"[2] and nothing more. Not that he did not get tired, even exhausted. By spending sometimes full days giving of his energy and power to those to whom he ministered,[3] exhaustion was inevitable; we see him fall asleep as he and the disciples crossed Galilee in a boat. But I think the difference was that the tiredness Jesus felt was not the result of stress or busyness. He remained relaxed and calm.

Why do we not hear so much about *this* Jesus preached in our churches? Maybe because, as I have already said, his calm, unhurried side is not made explicit in the text and sometimes goes unnoticed. Besides, we may ask, how could we possibly consider imitating that side of Jesus? Jesus was and is God, and such peace and intimacy with the Father was natural for him in a way that wouldn't be for us. Yes . . . but also no. Jesus would have had a predisposition to such a deep relationship, but we can forget that, in his birth, he gave up all rights to his status and power as God. He became fully human, like us, able to minister only by the power of the indwelling Holy Spirit that he received at his baptism in the Jordan.

But although he was fully human, Jesus' behavior was radically different from our own. *Our* Christian lives, if taken seriously, often add another layer to the busyness and stress of our lives as we try to use our energy and gifts for the betterment of our churches and the kingdom, addressing the needs we see around us.

Regardless, there's no question Jesus wants us to follow him into the way *he* lived. He tells us, in Eugene Peterson's *Message* translation of Matthew 11:28–30: "Walk with me and work with me—watch how I do it. Learn the unforced rhythms of grace. I

2. John 5:19.

3. Luke 8:46: Jesus said, "Someone touched me; I know that power has gone out from me."

won't lay anything heavy or ill-fitting on you. Keep company with me and you'll learn to live freely and lightly."

But how do we live freely and lightly? How did Jesus manage it? Eugene's words also suggest somehow a letting go, an abdication of the responsibility to move forward in pursuit of Christian maturity (and in the good works that James talks about and without which our faith is empty). Ironically, that abandonment is close to the truth and is what this book is about, an understanding that God put on my heart as my theological education drew to a close. In the intervening years, he has encouraged it to grow and mature in my mind until it was ready to write.

As I mentioned earlier, the answers to following Jesus, as he would wish us to, lie in Jesus' prayer life, which I will explore in the next chapter.

Chapter 1—Jesus' Prayer Life

SPRINKLED THROUGHOUT THE SYNOPTIC Gospels are six verses that point to perhaps four instances of Jesus' personal times of prayer. Given these verses don't *appear* to say anything profound or new, they are easy to overlook, although Luke obviously felt the solitary prayer times were important enough to mention on three occasions.

Some months back, Eugene Peterson, my former professor, came to mind for no apparent reason, and I tried to remember his favorite Bible verse. Why? I didn't know. I *did* know it concerned Jesus walking into the hills to pray. I read through the Gospels and discovered the verses listed below, which said much the same thing in various ways. The exercise didn't help me remember Eugene's favorite, possibly a verse from Mark, but the six verses stuck with me in the following days and weeks—until, one day, God opened them up to me and revealed a key, a way into the book I believed he wanted me to write. The verses, in chronological order, are:

1. Mark 1:35: *Very early in the morning, while it was still dark, Jesus got up, left the house and went off to a solitary place, where he prayed.* Luke 4:42: *At daybreak, Jesus went out to a solitary place.* The two Scriptures probably refer to the same event. Note that "wilderness" or "desert" replace "solitary place" in many translations.

2. Luke 5:16: *But Jesus often withdrew to lonely places and prayed.* Again, "wilderness" and "desert" are used in many translations.

1

3. Luke 6:12: *One of those days Jesus went out to a mountainside to pray, and spent the night praying to God.* This was the night before Jesus chose the twelve disciples.

4. Matthew 14:23: *After he had dismissed them, he went up on a mountainside by himself to pray. When evening came, he was there alone.* Mark 6:46: *After leaving them, he went up on a mountainside to pray.* Both passages probably refer to the same event after the feeding of the five thousand.

These verses, taken together, suggest a regular pattern of withdrawing to a place of solitude to pray; the word "often" appears in many translations of Luke 5:16. No surprise there. Jesus liked to pray. But these verses hold a gem of truth that points to a life following Jesus radically different from and simpler than most Christians in the Western evangelical world live today.

One significant aspect of these texts is the *time* Jesus spent in prayer. Although Luke 6:12 is the only instance where all-night prayer is mentioned, Jesus may have prayed through the night at other times. And even if he didn't, his times of prayer, requiring walking up into the desert or hills, were never a matter of the minutes by which we may measure our quiet times but of hours. Even so, it is unlikely he *talked* with God the whole time. Can you imagine Jesus doing that? Whether silent or spoken aloud, verbal prayer is often our limited view of what prayer is. I suggest that the time Jesus spent talking with God would probably have been brief. Remember when Jesus spoke on long prayers? He said, "When you pray, do not keep on babbling like pagans, for they think they will be heard because of their many words. Do not be like them, for your Father knows what you need before you ask him."[1]

God may have spoken to Jesus at times, though, again, I can't imagine the Father chattering on at length. Apart from an occasional nap, I think it probable that for much of these times of prayer, Jesus simply communed with God in periods of attentive silence.

1. Matthew 6:7–8.

Peterson wrote: "Jesus' nights of prayer suggest a 'being there' with God in silence and solitude,"[2] recognizing that, in the hours Jesus spent with God, verbal prayer was likely to give way to silent listening and keeping company with God.

I discovered something of the silence Jesus experienced in the small seaside town in Wales, where I began my new life as a Christian. A long beach stretched to a hill at the north end of the town, and given my love of mountains, I soon explored the cliffs that rose from the sea. With a little scrambling, I discovered a ledge I christened the "prayer rock," a comfortable shelf of slate hidden from the town and beach. There, I could gaze out at the sea with nothing to disturb my vision but for an occasional passing dolphin or seal. Regularly, I sat for an hour or more, my eyes stilled by the water, my mind filled with God in a loving silence.

Going back to the verses, as an illustration, I would like to delve a little deeper into Luke 6:12, where Jesus spent the night praying to God before choosing the disciples. Of the six verses, it is the only one suggesting a purpose for the time of prayer. Selecting the twelve would have been uppermost in Jesus' mind. We can only hazard a guess at what Jesus asked the Father. But I'm comfortable accepting that Jesus asked for the discernment the next day to choose the right men in accordance with God's will. And I'm equally comfortable with the idea that Jesus didn't need to ask anything of the Father. Either way, little needed to be said, and the importance of the night lay in the silent communion that nurtured the intimacy between Father and Son. Such closeness would ultimately lead to what my spiritual director calls "sanctified intuition"—the discernment, the "knowing" that Jesus would have had when he encountered each of the Twelve.

Mother Teresa was once asked, "When you pray, what do you say to God?"

Mother Teresa replied, "I don't say anything. I listen."

"Well, okay," the interviewer said, perplexed. "When God speaks to you, then, what does he say?"

---

2. Eugene Peterson, unpublished letter to the author, October 15, 1999.

3

"He doesn't say anything. He listens. And if you don't understand that, I can't explain it to you."

If *you* don't understand that, then you are not alone—neither did I once—but by the end of the book, I hope you will. The story is, I believe, a priceless example of the silent communion Jesus enjoyed with the Father.

Chapter 2—The Nature of Silence

SO WHAT IS THIS silence, this silent prayer that Jesus supposedly practiced in his times with the Father?

First, it does not *necessarily* refer to absolute silence. Instead, it describes a time when we (as I submit Jesus did) choose to be silent and surrender ourselves to God in an attentive, loving gaze, receiving his love in return. We allow him to have sovereignty over our time together—something we rarely do in church or our quiet times. And in that silence, what we experience, whether or not he speaks directly to us, is God's prerogative. For instance, my wife, Livia, and I once led a small group in silent prayer. God gave a friend, practicing it for the first time, a picture of herself walking by a river hand in hand with Jesus, leading her to tears of healing.

Second, for those who practice silent prayer, past and present, silence is the typical experience. Over the years, as I have spent an hour each morning sitting with God, I have *apparently* received nothing that I can recall but silence: no word, no pictures, no extraordinary sense of God's presence. Despite that, a day doesn't feel right if it hasn't begun with that hour, and I come away from it feeling as if I *have* spent time with him, quality time in which I have abandoned myself to his love.

Some authors write about what they call *listening prayer*, a different animal altogether. Although it requires a contemplative attitude, listening prayer is primarily a *doing* kind of prayer. It does not have the relaxed, passive attitude of silent prayer where we seek nothing but to love God. Here is one example of listening prayer connected with ministry.

When I was a young Christian, God led me into the ministry of inner healing and deliverance. After initial training, I became part of the church prayer ministry team. We would listen to those who came after the service with their wounds and problems while remaining attentive to God, asking him for discernment and direction in how to pray. Sometimes the person asking for prayer did not understand what was wrong with them. On one such occasion, accompanied by a ministry partner, I was asked to visit a woman in her home. The woman had significant emotional problems, but neither she nor her husband knew why. Not a good way to start such a time of ministry! Then God nudged me to look around the room we were in—nothing out of place—and whispered to me, "Perfectionism." I politely asked the woman if she thought she had any tendencies towards that problem, and her "yes" set the ball rolling, with God guiding all of us through a blessed time of healing for the woman.

Now is the perfect time to mention *contemplative prayer,* a name suggesting silence, which arose in medieval times. While contemplative prayer and silence are not synonymous, our faltering attempts at silent prayer are normally the first steps into contemplative prayer. The alternative is a "method" of contemplative prayer (e.g., Lectio Divina or Centering Prayer), where structured verbal prayers or meditation provide the way in. During contemplative prayer, our efforts are superseded by God's grace, and undistracted time with him becomes possible.

Today, we use many other names instead of contemplative prayer. I like "abiding prayer" because "abiding" is a biblical word and suggests the communion at its heart. But, throughout this book, I prefer to use "silent prayer" because that encompasses contemplative prayer and its humbler beginnings in attentive, loving silence before God. I will never use "silent prayer" to mean prayers of petition and intercession spoken in our minds.

I have no objections to the medieval name, but the words "contemplative" or "contemplation" are unnecessarily confusing, given they can be understood in many ways. The *Chambers Dictionary* defines the verb "to contemplate" as "to consider or look at attentively; to meditate on or study." Therein lies a source of confusion: many writers use the words "contemplation" and "meditation" interchangeably. However, when referring to "contemplative prayer," most writers on the spiritual life mean a silent and loving attentiveness to God where the mind is still and not meditating.

In exploring the nature of silent prayer, let's turn for a moment to the Word of God. Unfortunately, the Gospel verses do not use the word "silence." That may be a problem for some. How can I suggest that Jesus spent time in silence with his Father when none of the verses say that? To writers on the spiritual life and the biblical writers, prayer encompasses so much more than speaking to God. It includes meditation and abiding with God, and I will say more on this later. However, the criticism that "silence is not mentioned in the Gospels" is deeply rooted in some Christian attitudes to Scripture.

Christians have grown up with a Bible divided by chapters and verse numbers, although these divisions were not a part of the original manuscripts.[1] That system has provided convenience in accessing particular words and phrases but causes problems in interpretation with which many believers may not be familiar. There is the tendency to treat the Word as a manual from which we can extract an answer to every question we have about living the Christian life. Further, some assume that anything *not* in the Bible cannot be "biblical."

When God told me he wanted me to travel a third of the way around the world to Vancouver to study at a college I'd never heard of and for which I didn't have the finances, I had been a believer for fewer than three years. In his mercy, God spelled it out to me in at least thirty "signs" and coincidences, many of them revealing God's sense of humor. People in my church who knew me had no problem affirming the signs, except for one brother in Christ. Concerned that I'd received no confirmation from Scripture, he believed the other signs could not be trusted and be from God. When I told the vicar, he frowned, looked thoughtful for a

---

1. I recall Eugene Peterson saying that the introduction of chapters and verse numbers was the worst thing to happen to the Bible.

moment, and said, "Hmm. Correct me if I'm wrong, but I don't think Vancouver is mentioned in the Bible."

The Bible is nothing like an all-encompassing manual. Scripture consists of a diverse collection of God-breathed literature—from stories to poetry, from history to epistles, from proverbs to prophecy—which, when brought together, provides the history of God and his people.

But what concerns me more here is that much of Scripture is story and to be read as such. The story, however, can be forgotten or ignored when it is broken into verses. In narrative, much can be implied without being made explicit, and we can miss teaching and truth if our focus is on receiving wisdom through a verse or paragraph. For example, take the story of Jesus going up on the mountain to pray and sending the disciples off in the boat.[2] The next scene is the storm and Jesus walking on the water. The text doesn't describe him walking down the mountain, but we can safely assume he did.

The truth that Jesus spent many of his solitude hours in silent communion with his Father is implicit, as I will show in the next chapter where I place silence in the context of the Scriptures and Christian history.

Finally, if you are of the mind that whatever we call it, silent prayer smacks of "New Age" or the contemporary obsession with "mindfulness," remember that the truth is more likely the other way around. New Age and modern forms of popular spirituality are often corruptions that imitate genuine biblical, Christian practice that has a long history. And where meditation and contemplation always have Christ at their center, ancient Eastern religion and modern New Age equivalents attempt to focus on "nothing," emptying the mind.

2. Matthew 14:23.

Chapter 3—A Biblical and Historical Context

FOR MY FINAL COMPREHENSIVE paper at Regent College, I wrote on the practice of contemplative prayer and asked Eugene Peterson if he thought any evidence existed to support the idea that contemplative prayer was biblical. He replied: "There is plenty of indirect evidence. Paul's praying without ceasing suggests life as prayer, which I would call contemplative, Jesus' nights of prayer suggest a 'being there' with God in silence and solitude, Elijah at Horeb, John in the wilderness, Paul in Arabia are all suggestive of an immersion in silence and solitude in which God's presence is the overwhelming reality. . . . It doesn't take long to realize that the biblical material is contemplative through and through."[1]

For a Christian brought up in a society and church context in which silence plays little part, it's challenging to look at Peterson's summary of biblical heroes to recognize that for many if not most of God's prophets and other key biblical figures, extended time in the wilderness was a significant part of God's preparation and training for them. Here, separated from distractions, God spoke to them out of the silence. And through time with him, they grew in their faith. As Peterson said, they were immersed in a silence and solitude "in which God's presence [was] the overwhelming reality."[2] What a powerful way to grow in Christ.

Beyond Peterson's thoughts and conclusions, more specific evidence exists to suggest that something akin to contemplative prayer was practiced in the Bible. Writing on that subject,

1. Eugene Peterson, unpublished letter to the author, October 15, 1999.
2. Eugene Peterson, unpublished letter to the author, October 15, 1999.

Alexander Ryrie stated that "there is within the Old Testament a strand of spirituality, and a way of approaching God, which can be called contemplative."[3] He pointed to words and concepts which, when taken together, suggest that possibility. "Several Hebrew words which have to do with silence or quietness . . . carry the sense not only of silence but of waiting in silence or quiet expectation."[4] And, depending on the context, "to stand can . . . refer simply to *being* before God, to waiting in God's presence . . . in stillness and attention, . . . focusing on God alone."[5] Ryrie also proposed that to keep silent before God "was a way of acknowledging the holiness of God, and the mystery of his ways, and at the same time a sign of confidence and trust."[6] The ideas of silence and standing seem to indicate a different way of approaching God in prayer. They suggest that a form of contemplative prayer was inherent in the Old Testament writings.

When we turn to the New Testament, the only mention of teaching on prayer is found in Luke. "One day Jesus was praying in a certain place. When he finished, one of his disciples said to him, 'Lord, teach us to pray, just as John taught his disciples.'"[7] And so, Jesus taught the disciples the model of verbal prayer that we call the Lord's Prayer, the foundational prayer for Christians, which includes elements of petition, intercession, etc. If nothing else, Livia and I always pray the Lord's Prayer together each day. It makes no mention of silence, but then it does assume a loving attitude to God and the undergirding commandment to "love the Lord your God with all your heart and with all your soul and with all your strength and with all your mind."[8] And maybe Jesus did teach the disciples about silent prayer, but it wasn't recorded. We can be sure the Gospels do not include all of Jesus' conversations with them.

3. Ryrie, *Silent Waiting*, 1.

4. Ryrie, *Silent Waiting*, 21 citing TDOT, vol. III, 262–64.

5. Ryrie, *Silent Waiting*, 27.

6. Ryrie, *Silent Waiting*, 130.

7. Luke 11:1–4.

8. Luke 10:27.

The end of the Bible didn't signify the end of God teaching and interacting with his people. The Bible appears to close at a convenient point following Jesus' ascension and the beginnings of the early church, but God continued to teach and guide his people without pause. While the canon of Scripture is foundational to our Christian faiths, we also need to learn from the followers of Jesus throughout history. The reading set for my first course at Regent College came as a shock. It was all Catholic, written just after the Reformation, though I would later read books that went as far back as the fourth century. To my delight, what I found was a richness to the reading that I had seldom seen in contemporary works, a richness that revealed an implicit love for God that didn't have to be clarified.

Now is not the time for a discussion of Christian history. But it is important to note that Emperor Constantine was responsible for the institutionalization of the church and for it becoming the dominant religion of the Roman Empire during his reign (306–337 AD). But, while it removed the threat of persecution, the Christianity he represented was often nominal, with the rich and powerful dominating the church. In reaction to this, those seeking God more earnestly left for a life in the desert free of distractions. These early Christian hermits, known today as the Desert Fathers, began to gather with a common aim, and monasticism was born. In the thousand years to the Reformation, many of the writings coming out of monasticism point in the same direction: to intimacy with God and contemplative prayer. Nearly all such writings are available today, in various translations—amazing considering the shelf life of books published today. Many have become "classics," like *The Cloud of Unknowing* (author unknown) and *Revelations of Divine Love* by Julian of Norwich, both written in the fourteenth century. And together, all these writings suggest the direction and maybe inspiration of God, guiding believers deeper into intimacy with him.

Prayer is, and always was, primarily about relationship with God, the subject to which I now turn.

Chapter 4—Relationship with God

IN THE BEGINNING, "GOD created man in his own image, in the image of God he created them; male and female he created them."[1] God created us for one primary purpose, that we might enjoy a relationship with him. God is relational in himself. Father, Son, and Spirit live continuously in abundant mutual love and respect. We were created that we might partake of that overflowing love between them and enter into the dance of the Trinity.

For a fictional representation of this, I recommend the book, *The Shack* by William P. Young, or the movie of the same name. While the story is a fantasy, and some aspects of it may be theologically challenging, Young represents the Trinity's relationship dynamics in a way that provides much to reflect on. However fictional they are, stories can sometimes present us with truth more directly and profoundly than theological statements, getting under our defenses. Why else did Jesus often reveal truth through the telling of parables?

The fact that God created us in his image affirms the love he has for us. Theologians have argued *how* he made us in his image, but perhaps that misses the point. Had God created us for anything other than a loving relationship with him, he would not have shaped us in such a sacred and humbling way, in effect using his DNA.

As Christians, we assume that we live in a relationship with God. But what should a relationship founded on love and friendship look like? In our lifetimes, we form hundreds of relationships, but not all are alike. Most are utilitarian, based on what

1. Genesis 1:27.

others (e.g., doctors, accountants, work colleagues, etc.) can do for us or what we can do for them. In this book, we are interested only in personal relationships based on love and friendship, and, by their nature, they are an end in themselves and what God created us for. They should serve no useful purpose. Sadly, we sometimes marry because we believe our spouse will make us happy, a subtle form of utilitarianism that often leads to disappointment. Far happier are those who enter marriage to give and receive the joy and love of the relationship.

So what does our relationship with God look like from this perspective? He exhorts us not to worry about our lives (Matthew 6:25), but to seek his kingdom first, and he will supply all our needs. He wants us to come to him with all our concerns and needs, and we do. We fill our quiet times with requests for ourselves and for those we love or events and circumstances we wish to see changed. We call them "petition" and "intercession." In general, they are the summation of what we bring to God in prayer. When we pray, we ask God to do something or provide something. And there is nothing wrong with that. God desires that we pray so we can relate to him and grow in that relationship. But if that is all our relationship with God amounts to, it looks primarily transactional and one-sided.

As previously mentioned, Jesus told us that the greatest commandment is to "love the Lord your God with all your heart and with all your soul and with all your strength and with all your mind."[2] But what does that look like? From my perspective, our modern model of Christian devotion falls a long way short of this high bar. On Sundays, we do come together in church to worship God and raise our voices in praise to him for twenty or thirty minutes, thanking him for who he is and what he does. But, to be strictly honest with ourselves, it often makes us feel good too, and our motivation may be divided.

There are other problems to consider. Close and intimate relationships are not founded on communication alone, especially when it is primarily one-sided. At a time when text and email allow

2. Luke 10:27.

instant communication like never before, it is interesting to hear that loneliness among the young is higher than ever. Real personal relationships require communion as much as communication, quality time together with no purpose other than to know one another better. Knowing someone is not merely knowing *about* them—about obtaining information regarding their interests and needs—but something far more mystical and undefinable. Knowing *about* God from our study of the Scriptures cannot replace knowing God through extended direct contact. Ironically, we can come to know someone well while knowing little *about* them.

I am an avid film watcher and, unless we have something else going on, Livia and I usually relax together in the evening, taking turns choosing which film to watch. Thankfully, often the choice suits us both, though not always! Whatever we watch, I like to check out the reviews and, on occasions, I read one that draws attention to the on-screen chemistry or lack of it between two actors. Chemistry may not be exactly the same thing, but it does point to the mystery of what makes a relationship work. Dating agencies can pair up potentially suitable partners according to location and interests, but they cannot predict how the "chemistry" will work, if at all. Mystery lies at the heart of close relationships.

Often, the older a married couple gets, the less they need to talk, and they find contentment in simply being together. To the observer, nothing is happening, whereas *much* is happening in the communion of two souls or spirits. Likewise, in the silent worship of God, we can meet and commune with him, going to him for him alone and not with any other agenda, coming to know God and not just know *about* God. When we do that, I believe that blesses him.

The essence of prayer is relationship. When we look at the times Jesus spent alone in prayer to God, does it not make more sense that verbal prayer would quickly give way to an extended time of silent communion?

Chapter 5—The Context of Prayer

I BECAME EXCITED WHEN I found out my church planned to take us through a Bible study on prayer, only to be later disappointed to find that the proposed book was on *prayers* (plural), specific requests of God found in Scripture. As I have noted, most churchgoers today would think of prayer in terms of petition or intercession, whether spoken out loud or silently within ourselves. But, as we have seen, it has a much broader definition both in Scripture and in Christian history and includes meditative prayer and silent or contemplative prayer, which eschews any form of words—spoken or silent. Where silent prayer "fits" within the whole context of prayer, we can helpfully see in at least two different models.

In the sixteenth century, a Carmelite nun, Teresa of Avila, wrote several books that, together, amount to a systematic theology of prayer. Eugene Peterson regarded her as equally important in church history as Luther and Calvin and acknowledged that her writings (together with those of her close friend, St. John of the Cross) had educated him in the ways of the spiritual life that his training as a pastor had failed to do.

The Interior Castle, her most famous work, describes seven levels or "mansions" of spiritual growth and prayer that increasingly lead to greater intimacy with and relational knowledge of God. The first three are the active mansions of verbal prayer and meditative prayer that correspond to the experiences of prayer enjoyed by most modern Christians, many of whom will not pass beyond the third level in their lifetimes. Some Christians may have experiences of the fourth and fifth levels but return to the third because they have no mentors to guide them, and we do not teach about the passive mansions in the church.

The final four are the passive mansions of contemplative prayer, where we will progress as we abandon ourselves more and more to God's control and the experience of the silence and mystery of prayer. But it is prayer in which we increasingly find ourselves, ironically, closer and closer to God. To begin with, contemplative prayer is filled with distractions that we have to brush aside. Even after years of practicing silence with God, while gazing at him, my mind can suddenly turn to what I need to buy at the supermarket later in the day! However, with perseverance, we will find ourselves in periods of true stillness and silence where the only reality is God.

The Interior Castle is a beautiful book, though not easy to read. Its language is mystical, and it is not written in an orderly fashion. Teresa wrote it more as a journal of her spiritual experiences at the request of her superiors. In contrast, *Mansions of the Heart* by R. Thomas Ashbrook is a systematic and down-to-earth account of Teresa's teachings and much more accessible to modern Christians. Peterson wrote the preface from which I have drawn his comments above. Having undertaken a great deal of spiritual reading for my degree, this book is a favorite and, I believe, a must-read for pastors who want to understand and help guide the spiritual lives of their congregants and by other Christians who aspire to know God deeper.

The second model comes from James Houston in his seminal book on prayer, *The Transforming Friendship*. Houston proposed a circle divided into quadrants representing all types of prayer. He suggested that, in our maturing spiritual lives, we should come to experience the full circle, moving clockwise from verbal prayer through meditative prayer finally to silent and contemplative prayer. The right side of the circle (verbal and meditative prayer) represents prayer to the God who has revealed himself through Scripture, creation, the sacraments, etc. and corresponds with the first three of Teresa's mansions.[1]

---

1. For those interested in pursuing the subject, this is known as kataphatic prayer, in contrast to apophatic contemplative prayer. In addition, Houston's upper quadrants relate to prayer associated with the mind, the lower ones,

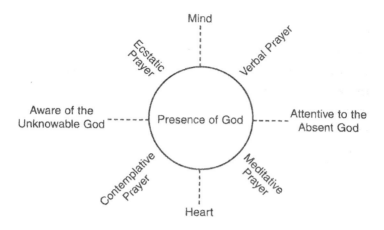

Houston wrote that we "also experience God as unknowable, as Moses found when a cloud hid God from sight. Then we focus in awe and wonder upon the great mystery of God. Paradoxically, it is at times when we sense his great mystery that he seems to be present with us in the most intimate way possible."[2] In Houston's model, prayer to the unknowable God is found on the left side of the circle, which corresponds with the passive mansions of Teresa's model. Contemplative prayer affirms that God can only be truly known not through words but through relationship, being together.

When I was a young Christian, God put his arms around me and hugged me as I sat on a beach. Strange words, but I can think of no other way to put it. The sense of his love for me was so intense and overpowering, almost unbearable, that I cannot find any words to express how it felt. But nearly thirty years later, the memory still affects me. Looking back, I imagine God may have given me a brief taste of what his love will feel like in heaven, too much for my earthly body to receive comfortably. "Love" as a word is so inadequate, and I recognize that whatever words I try to come up with, they only diminish the experience.

---

prayer of the heart.

2. Houston, *Transforming Friendship*, 254.

Houston labels the final upper left quadrant of the circle as "ecstatic prayer," a name for experiences of God that transcend what we consider normal and for which we cannot prepare. Houston stated: "Ecstasy is the true climax of our friendship with God in prayer. The word *ecstasy* comes directly from a Greek word which literally means to be 'taken out of ourselves.'"[3] Being "slain in the Spirit" would come under this heading, as would my encounter on the beach, experiences that might usually be confined to the upper mansions of passive prayer.

It is important to note that these are models, and our progress in prayer, *may* take us steadily through the mansions or around Houston's circle. But as the above story illustrates, God is always sovereign, and an experience of the sixth mansion may happen to someone based in the first three. Or someone in the first verbal quadrant of prayer may suddenly find him or herself in the last ecstatic quadrant, encountering God in the most intimate of ways.

3. Houston, *Transforming Friendship*, 269.

Chapter 6—Ministry

I HAVE SAID NOTHING so far about ministry. Where does that fit? Sitting with God is fine, but what about the work to be done out in the world, the hurting to be ministered to, and the lost to be saved? In every church I've attended, ministry and mission have been seen as the main priorities. Doing good works for God usually stands preeminent over our prayerful relationship with him.

On a train journey, I once found myself sitting opposite an older lady—I will call her Sarah—immersed in a Christian devotional book. After introducing myself to this sister in Christ, she shared her passion for intercession and saw herself as a prayer warrior. I became increasingly concerned as the lovely, godly lady talked about the many hours she prayed each day, apparently *driven* by the needs she saw in the world around her. When I told her of my degree and the final paper I had written on contemplative prayer, she asked me what that was. I described it to her, and a look of horror dawned on her face. She finally asked me, "But isn't that a terrible waste of time?" Why would we spend time with God, merely to enjoy his presence, when there is so much to be done?

The idea has a long history. Recall in the Bible that Martha "had a sister called Mary, who sat at the Lord's feet listening to what he said. But Martha was distracted by all the preparations that had to be made. She came to him and asked, 'Lord, don't you care that my sister has left me to do the work by myself? Tell her to help me!' 'Martha, Martha,' the Lord answered, 'you are worried and upset about many things, but only one thing is needed. Mary has chosen what is better, and it will not be taken away from her.'"[1]

---

1. Luke 10:38–42.

My memory has been kind to me in that I can't remember how I replied to Sarah's comment. But I squirm when I picture her getting off the train at the next stop, defeated looking, trampled on. What had I done? The following Sunday, I attended an Anglican church near where I was staying, and who should come in but Sarah. I attempted to hide, but she had already seen me and, with a smile (no doubt fixed on!), came over to introduce me to her friend. I was embarrassed and lost for something to say, but, bless her, she rescued me. "Thank you for sharing with me on the train," she said, "I needed to hear it." Affirming words . . . but I still squirm at the memory!

The emphasis on ministry is not so surprising. In the Western world, we are raised in a society where our prime identity is wrapped up in what we do, how we make our livings. When we meet someone new, we ask them their name and what they do and make judgments accordingly. The need for an identity follows us into the Christian world, where we will probably only find security and identity when we are doing something for God and the church. Our identity *should* be in Christ, apart from anything we do, but this is the ideal situation of the whole, healed, and mature Christian who knows God's love at the deepest level of his or her being. Most Christians don't possess this kind of security, many having grown up in less than perfect family settings where parental figures have distorted how we see God and where trusting him is by no means natural. In consequence, many if not most believers find identity primarily in what they do for God.

Returning home to the UK after graduating from Regent College, I found myself caring for my mother, who had dementia, and God told me I would look after her until she died. This was not the glorious world-changing ministry I, like I suspect most fellow graduates, had anticipated. For two and a half years, I stayed with her, and by the time she passed away, I was burned out and on the edge of depression. With her home quickly sold, God led me to take a sabbatical in a Christian community in the Austrian Alps, where I slowly healed. But what was strange was that I no longer possessed any trappings of a typical modern life: no home to return to and few belongings beyond what I had with me; no job or even career awaiting me, my field of work having moved on while I was away studying. And, on sabbatical, I had no responsibilities or duties within the community except "to be." In short, I'd been stripped of any chance to find my identity in what I *did*. Moreover, while I had a little money from my mother's estate, I had no idea what God would want me to do next or where in the world that would be, all ties now severed. By God's grace, despite an odd situation to experience, I found myself at peace and knew my identity was truly in him, a loving God for whom I needed to do nothing.

But regardless of the health of our relationship with God, I believe we all look for identity in what we do. It's somehow written into our DNA. As I write this, I'm questioning whether I will seek to find an identity as a writer! The temptation is there.

For those with distorted or false images of God, particularly those relating to the Father, ministry and other such works for God can become a way of appeasing or pleasing him. Where we see him as the Old Testament God of wrath, our works become a form of sacrifice to keep his anger from us. Alternatively, they can be a way of winning God's love and affection, a way of pleasing him. God is a God of love, but we may feel that we still have to earn that love. That's what we may believe deep down.

Pelagius, a theologian of the fourth century, was credited with the heresy of salvation by works, that we are saved by the good works we do, rather than by grace. I seem to recall James Houston suggesting that, for most of us, while we know in our minds we are saved by grace and faith in Jesus Christ, deep down we are "practical Pelagians," living our Christian lives as if our salvation depended on ourselves and what we do for God. Though none of us would readily admit to these models of distortion, many if not most believers subscribe to them at a deep or subconscious level. For further study on these distortions of how we see and relate to God, I recommend *With: Reimagining the Way You Relate to God* by Skye Jethani, a challenging but helpful read in determining how our relationship with God might be skewed.

Another reason for the emphasis on ministry and mission over relationship with God, is the recognition that there is so much need around us. As I shared earlier, Sarah attempted to carry that heavy burden herself in prayer. We are surrounded not only by the unsaved, but also the sick and the broken, even within our churches. Believers don't come to faith nicely cleaned up, but with most of their baggage intact and now, under God's influence, more likely to surface after being long-buried. We are much in need of each other's prayers. However, the stark but also freeing truth I may have shared with Sarah is that God can accomplish everything he wants to without us. And some of my stories show that. He chooses to use us for the sake of relationship, ours with him and with each other.

The problem with the emphasis on ministry in so many churches is that it can become almost idolatrous. That's a strong word to use, so let me explain. When asked by the Pharisees which was the greatest commandment in the Law, Jesus replied: "'Love the Lord your God with all your heart and with all your soul and with all your mind.' This is the first and greatest commandment. And the second is like it: 'Love your neighbor as yourself.'"[2]

Ministry and mission would come under the second commandment. Sadly, I see little evidence in the church to indicate we take the first commandment even remotely seriously. The words themselves set a high bar, suggesting an all-consuming effort on our part to love God. Fifteen minutes of petition and intercession in the morning doesn't come close. We have forsaken our first love and placed the second commandment over the first, perhaps making ministry an idol above God. We give it a title and set it apart from other activities of the church or things we ourselves do as Christians. But that wasn't the case for Jesus. Ministry was simply part of how he lived, the natural outpouring of communion with the Father and doing his Father's will.

In a letter to Dom Bede Griffiths in 1951, C. S. Lewis summarized what he saw as the existence of a universal law relating to first and second things: "Put first things first and we get second

2. Matthew 22:37–39.

things thrown in: put second things first and we lose both first and second things. We never get, say, even the sensual pleasure of food at its best when we are being greedy."[3]

By putting ministry above deepening our relationships with God, we end up with a shallower relationship with God and the lesser fruits of a ministry not necessarily blessed and empowered by him. Put a deep relationship with God first and, among countless other blessings, he guides us into ministry that he blesses and empowers. Jesus put the Father first, before his ministry. Indeed, he had no ministry without the Father. "The Son can do nothing by himself; he can do only what he sees his Father doing, because whatever the Father does the Son also does. For the Father loves the Son and shows him all he does" (John 5:19–20).

We have to get it the right way round by focusing on God first and foremost. Intimacy with God together with our identity in Christ and knowledge of his love for us, both experienced at the heart level, will bring everything else in their wake. "But seek first his kingdom and his righteousness, and all these things will be given to you as well" (Matthew 6:33). "All these things" includes not just material goods but *everything*, including the ministry God has for us. In the chapter on fruits, I share a story where, by being focused on my healing and increased intimacy with God, ministry happened, naturally and organically with no effort on my part. If we want to see people come to Christ, if we want to see healing of the broken, if we want to see revival, then our focus should be on intimacy with God first, not ministry. Ministry will happen naturally. Now let's look at how we can place our focus on intimacy with God.

3. Hooper, *Collected Letters*, 111.

Chapter 7—Practicing Silence

WE PUT OUR INTIMACY with God first by learning to abide with him in prayer. It is all well and good to talk about silence and contemplative prayer, but what does one do, and what does it look like to someone used only to verbal prayer?

Let me begin by saying that the shift from a position of perceived control to one of complete abandonment to God will possibly feel somewhat alien and challenging to some believers. Because of the distortions in the way we see God that I spoke of in the last chapter, we may not trust God enough to open ourselves up to him in such an intimate way. But, by God's grace, any misgivings quickly can pass when we step out in faith to just be with God.

While there are no rules, many classical and modern writers have written on contemplative prayer and silence, and their writings can provide a guide. But I would like to share the things that have been helpful in my own experience.

To begin with, start small. Make sure that you are sitting somewhere comfortable and quiet where you won't be disturbed. Set aside no more than ten minutes for the silent prayer, five minutes if you prefer. And perhaps set a quiet alarm, so you won't be wondering how much time has passed and be tempted to look at your watch. The time will *feel* much longer than it is. Don't go into silence "cold." First, spend some time in the Word, maybe reading a passage out loud, which takes up more of your attention and clears the atmosphere of anything that might distract you. You can be sure the enemy does not want you doing anything that might engender deeper intimacy with God. Then follow your time in the Word with some verbal prayer, finally offering God your undivided silence for ten minutes to use as he pleases and asking him to bless the time.

Close your eyes and focus your attention on God, gazing at him by faith with love and attentiveness. Imagine it, perhaps, as Sunday-morning worship without the music and words. This is not a time of thinking *about* God. Your mind should be still but *not* empty (a popular misconception). Instead it should be *full*, full of God. You are simply looking upon him with love in the way you would with a loved one. Your breathing should slow down, and your body relax.

Inevitably, the distractions will come. Let me stress that. For a few seconds, you'll be doing fine, and then your mind wanders. You may not even realize it at first. What follows is key. Do not be disappointed, frustrated, or angry. These emotions will not be helpful here. Maintain your slow breathing and relaxed state and use a biblical word or short phrase to bring yourself back to God. I whisper, "Father." Choose whatever is most meaningful to you. Distractions will come, time and time again, but it is important *not* to think of this as failure. It is easy to do; we are so performance-oriented and want to please him. Remember that we *do* please him before we even get out of bed in the morning. Are we not delighted with our children without them having to try to please us? Having said that, I believe God is particularly blessed by us offering such time to him that is not about needs and wants.

Although it is nice to experience undistracted silence, what happens during the time given over to silence is largely irrelevant. Sometimes I have gone to sleep. It doesn't matter. I felt guilty at first until I realized that I had given God sovereignty over that time and that, so long as I tried to stay focused on him, whatever happened was willed or allowed by him, even the distractions. That's the most important lesson: *don't judge your silent time with God*. In time, distractions will increasingly give way to more protracted periods of silence. You might want to end your ten minutes of silence with verbal prayers of petition and intercession. Once we learn to abide with God in silence, we find that we don't need to use as many words.

Again, these are only guidelines to what you will probably experience. But God is sovereign over these times and will do whatever he wants, and you might suddenly experience his presence profoundly. With practice, as you progress through silence into Teresa of Avila's passive mansions of prayer, profound encounters with God become far more likely. But it is as well not to evaluate our times with God according to what we "feel."

Feelings can be an inaccurate gauge of the spiritual realm in such times. Ironically, those times when God feels far away can be times when he is closer than ever, so close that our senses overload and shut down, and time flies by. Our physical senses are designed to perceive the material world around us, not the spiritual world. It is the Holy Spirit who enables us to learn to sense God. We usually think of prayer as an exchange of information. In contemplative silence, the exchange is love itself.

When you are comfortable with ten minutes, then extend it as long as you are able. My quiet time in the morning is an hour of which perhaps ten minutes is Bible reading and verbal prayer, the rest is silence. Given the hours Jesus devoted to communing with the Father, I would like it to be more. While I continue to have distractions, there are more times when I experience complete stillness and silence.

You might well ask why anyone would persevere, spending long periods in distracted silence when they don't feel God's presence. A good question. Here, I would point you to the next chapter on the fruits of such prayer. Suffice to say, it is a highlight of my day, and I miss it when it is not there. And while God's presence isn't obvious or profound, apart from a quiet sense of peace, I am aware at times he is at work in me and also of the steady drip-feed of his love into me. It is, to all who practice it, deeply satisfying. In a beautiful way, you could describe it as addictive! Interestingly, when I recently told my spiritual director that I rarely felt God's presence, he argued that I probably do. That it had become so "normal" to me that anything but an extraordinary experience of God went unnoticed.

My wife was quick to suggest that while I have the luxury of time to sit with God for an hour in the day, many people with children and jobs struggle to manage the shortest of quiet times in their days. That's a fair point, although I won't let you off the hook just yet.

Let me tell you a story. A professor at Regent College invited a fellow student and me to walk early each day around a park situated halfway between our homes in suburban Vancouver. The professor needed the exercise, and he felt our spiritual conversations would benefit us. They did and blessed me. On my bookshelves, I have a journal in which I jotted down the spiritual gems he had come out with as we walked. But my health was poor, and I soon found that the early mornings left me exhausted, and my days were not as fruitful study-wise. Eventually, I told the professor that I couldn't manage our walks anymore, sad though I was. I remember his reply very well, words that have challenged me ever since, for example, when I'm forced to choose between spending time with God or playing my guitar. He said, "You'll do what you consider most important." That's all. I still gave up the walks, but "what is most important?" was a good question to ask myself and one that God brings to mind more often than I would like.

So I will ask you whether in your busy life you have time to watch television for an hour. It's not a fair question. Sitting on the sofa with your spouse in front of the TV may well be the only downtime you get to share with him or her. But the statement the professor made still doesn't go away. Ask yourself how important God is to you.

There is, however, another solution to finding extended time for God, and I will return to it in chapter 9. It is not ideal; practicing both is ideal. But in a life beset by busyness, it is an alternative.

Chapter 8—The Fruits of Silent Prayer

GOD IS AT WORK in us all the time, unseen and unknown to us, slowly transforming us into the likeness of Jesus Christ, exhibiting the presence, gifts, and fruit of the Holy Spirit. No fruits of silent prayer are unique to this spiritual disciple alone. God works in many ways to transform us. But I would suggest that the fertile spiritual soil of silence provides more abundant fruit than most other disciplines in certain areas. So most of what follows is subjective but founded on the experiences of those who have walked with God in silence over the last two thousand years and written about those experiences.

Love & Identity

Jesus loves me, this I know.
For the Bible tells me so.

When I hear them, the words of this classic children's hymn leave me feeling sad, for they echo the situation of possibly most Christians today who know Jesus loves them, know God loves them, as a theological truth. And they know *about* God, rather than knowing God experientially. Studying the Bible is, or should be, an essential part of every Christian's life. Although Paul was talking about the Old Testament in his letter to Timothy, his words apply to all the Bible. "All Scripture is God-breathed and is useful for teaching, rebuking, correcting and training in righteousness" (2 Timothy 3:16). However, if we only approach the Word to study it, to gain understanding and information, as so many of us do, we will come to know *about* Jesus and *about* God, and that's not enough. Not to know them in relationship, not to receive their love.

Do you know God or just *about* God? Do you know and experience God's love or just about it? It's easy to hide the truth from ourselves. If you don't know for sure, try asking yourself some simple questions. If, for months on end, God were to remove all sense of his presence from you, would you still know his love for you, or would you have doubts? If, then, you became seriously ill, what now? If our circumstances dictate what we believe about God's love for us, then the chances are we don't so much know God as we know *about* him. We don't live in the light of God's love for us; we simply know *about* it.

Knowing about God is not enough. Not enough to find our identity in Christ. Not enough to sustain the challenges of a Christian pilgrimage through a life beset with problems and pain. And not enough to live out an authentic relationship with God, his intention for us from the beginning. Some Christians, I know, are so broken that they don't even recognize his love for them even when they read it in the Bible. But most Christians, in my experience, believe that God loves them at this cerebral level. I recently asked our next-door neighbor, a retired pastor, how many people in the body of Christ he thought knew God and his love for them at the heart level. He paused for a moment and then replied, sadly, "A minority." Sad indeed!

While studying at Regent College, I met a pastor who had taken two weeks off to take a course at the college. At first glance, he seemed a dauntingly godly man, rising at 4:00 am each day to pray for several hours before moving into the rest of the day. At this level, he impressed all those who met him. But it didn't take long for the reality of his situation to come out. He couldn't relax, even away from his church, and was close to burning out. His church was failing, and nothing he did seemed to help its demise. And his seemingly devout prayers each morning were, unfortunately, not those of a godly man, at peace in God's presence. They were those of a man desperate to see his church pull through and to win God's love and affection. It turned out that his father had been a pastor, so busy that his son had to make an appointment to see him, and he saw personal success as the way to reach his father—and, as it happened, his "heavenly" Father too.

Burnout among pastors is common these days, and I believe one of its root causes is not knowing God's love at the heart level. Such knowledge should allow a pastor not to fall prey to trying to please God, because he already knows he doesn't have to lift a finger to please his heavenly Father. Nor ought pandering to the congregation's expectations be a temptation; if he knows God's love, he won't seek to win popularity from his church but do only what he feels led to do.

We need not only to know *about* God and *about* his love for us; we need to experience it at the heart level. And, as a wise person once said, "The distance between the head and the heart is a long one." God can, and often does, break through our daily lives to reveal his love for us in a profound way. I was blessed to experience deeply God's love for me in a Damascus Road-type conversion, but two years later, as I shared earlier, I experienced God's overwhelming love for me *physically*—one huge step beyond the heart level—when he put his arms around me as I sat on a beach. So, yes, God can break through with a revelation of his love. But we can make space for him—indeed, we *need* to make time for him in our daily devotional time, in the midst of our busy lives, when he can reveal his love for us. Though he broke through on that day, I was sitting alone, perhaps not focused on him but certainly in a receptive place.

To sit in silence with him creates the space for us to receive his love. It's a time when we are no longer in control but abandoned to him and his ways. We cannot predict what he will do or say, and for some of us, that is hard because of our past lives. Like the Israelites at Mount Sinai, we are often afraid of hearing directly from God, afraid of a personal encounter. In nearly thirty years of Christian life, I've heard from God so many times, some of which have changed my life completely. He knows what's best for us more than we do, and looking back, I've heard nothing from him that has resulted in anything less than a blessed life.

Presence

Jesus had a presence that attracted people to him. Obviously, his miracles drew crowds to him, as did his teaching, the likes of which they had not heard before. But more than that, I believe his face shone with the presence of the Holy Spirit. Isaiah 53:2 suggests that he was not handsome: "Nothing in his appearance that we should desire him." But, as someone who spent so much time with the Father, how could he not possess something of the radiance that Moses experienced when on Mount Sinai talking to God?[1]

Paul exhorts us in Ephesians 5:18 to "be filled with the Spirit." And many other verses affirm this. But what is our capacity to receive the Spirit, and is it as large as it could be? When we become Christians, we put our lives under the lordship of Christ, but to what extent do we normally submit our lives to him? Or, to put it another way, how much of us does the Spirit have?

Many of us lead divided lives. On the one hand, we may have successful jobs for which we are well trained and where our professional capability gives us little need for dependence on God. That's not our fault. We are in control of what we do, or at least believe it and give the impression that we are. Only when we are *not* doing that—when things become more complicated, when we are home with our spouses and children, our friends and church lives, where we are not so "professionally" equipped and in control, and where interpersonal relationships *do* require help from God—do we become more submissive to him.

When we enter a long time of silence with God, we are surrendering our control, giving it to him, abandoning ourselves to his will during that time. It is not a comfortable thought for people living in the twenty-first century. Control is important to all of us, though we might not voice it. And that applies to everyone in the church too. Gradually, this abandonment to God, when it becomes a habit, allows us to give more space to the Holy Spirit. And in doing so, our witness becomes stronger. And lest you think the degree

---

1. Exodus 34:29.

of radiance that Jesus and Moses exhibited was not for the likes of modern Christians, let me humbly share a personal story.

As a new Christian, I attended a residential week for those wanting to learn how to minister inner healing. Besides receiving teaching, the organizers required each attendee to undergo several hours of inner healing themselves. Somewhat naively, I might say stupidly now, I prayed that God would do with me whatever he wanted no matter what the cost! The result was I received far more healing and deliverance than the leaders were comfortable with, and they were deeply concerned for me at the end.

Leaving the facility, I felt disoriented, as though wearing someone else's glasses, but recovered by the following morning before my journey home. I was tired and not particularly sociable. Nevertheless, on a busy mainline train, several people engaged me in conversation, and one man even moved seats to talk to me. I didn't think much about it at the time. On a quieter second train, an anxious young mother with a newborn baby called to me across the carriage and asked if I minded her moving to my table. We didn't talk, but she seemed much happier there, sat opposite me. When I got home, I discovered from a friend that two friends of hers had been on the same train and, in their words, had not been able to take their eyes off me the whole journey, my face apparently radiant. I wasn't aware of them, and to this day, I don't know where they sat. But when they asked my friend where I'd been, and she reluctantly told them I'd "been away to spend time with God," they gasped and replied, "That would explain it." And soon they gave their lives to God. I wonder how many others on the trains were affected by what the Holy Spirit was doing through me.

Though an unusual experience, seeing my unintentional "witness" from the other side proved to be enlightening, confirming to me that giving God control, abandoning ourselves to him, produces ministry and witness that goes beyond what we can imagine. And on an ongoing basis, how much of my more modest daily abandonment to God in silence quietly witnesses to those I encounter each day?

Our witness can also be to other believers. I also recall being taken aback by a question put to me while at Regent College. As I gathered my things at the end of a lecture, a young woman two rows in front caught my eye and asked, "You know him, don't you?" It was clear who she was referring to. I was so stumped I'm not sure I replied, and she didn't seem to need an answer. She disappeared before I could question her. Why did she ask? What did she see? The memory still humbles me.

I'm sure many of you will have had similar experiences and am convinced that, unbeknownst to us, all of us who are Christians, born again of the Spirit, witness to those around us to one degree or another.

Active Contemplation

In 1 Thessalonians 5:17, Paul exhorted the Thessalonians to pray continually or without ceasing. What that means in practice may be debated since, as we have seen, prayer is wider than verbal petitionary or intercessory prayer. What is clear is that spending time in silent communion with God increasingly results in that communion being brought out of the quiet time into daily life. Active contemplation is my own term, though it may have been used elsewhere, for the increasing level of internal stillness, peace, and silence that pervades those who regularly spend their time with God in silence. Because of the busyness and distractions of the day, God may not always be central in our thoughts, but we become open to him speaking to us. I think of him being in my peripheral vision and hearing, requiring little effort to refocus on him.

Slowing Down

There's no doubt that practicing contemplative prayer leads to a much-needed slowing down from the rush of modern life to a speed more in line with God that comes with increasing peace and stillness. Debilitating health issues prove to be a blessing to me in at least one way: they keep me at home, away from the normal workday stress encountered by most people. And I experience this fruit externally as well as internally. In everything I do, I'm rarely hurried or rushed. Nevertheless, stillness and peace can be experienced as an inner tranquillity, even in the midst of external busyness.

God's Operating Theater

As I stated at the beginning of the chapter, from the moment we accept Christ into our lives until we take our last breaths, God is sanctifying us, transforming us into the image of his Son, readying us for heaven. The process goes on, largely unseen. But, when we surrender our control to God in times of silence and contemplative prayer, it is easier for him to work on us.

Several times, following a time of silence, he has given me a picture of myself laid out, calm and at peace, on an operating table with a drip feed attached. With the picture has come the understanding that because I'd chosen for this hour to surrender myself to God, he can do far more spiritual "surgery" on me than when I'm on the move or wrestling with him. And when this surgery is not taking place, he is still dripping into me a potent solution of his love and peace and the fruits of the Spirit. I have often finished my quiet time with the strange feeling that something has changed in me, that God has tweaked something, but I can never say what it is. I just know that he's been at work, uninterrupted.

Healing/Wholeness

I have been involved in the ministry of inner healing and deliverance since I became a believer. Over those years, I have seen many people healed of their brokenness by having someone minister to their wounded memories. But I've also come to know that while he doesn't always heal our physical health issues, God *does* heal our psychological problems if we allow him to—he wants as little as possible to interfere with an intimate relationship with him—and that extended times of abandoned silence with him provide a wonderful opportunity.

I witnessed this on one occasion when ministering to a teenage girl with a terrible history of abuse. God asked me to have her stand while my ministry partner and I prayed for her. Within seconds she was "slain in the Spirit," and we gently lowered her to the ground and covered her with a blanket. The girl was "out" for thirty minutes, and all we could do was watch and pray in tongues, feeling inadequate. That was all it took for God to heal her of substantial past wounds. A week later, I barely recognized her in church.

Much of God's emotional healing can go unheralded, and we may only notice it months or years later. But God can also bring healing by breaking into our times of silence. I already shared one such example in the first chapter when a friend, practicing silent prayer for the first time, received a picture of herself walking by a river hand in hand with Jesus. Livia experienced something even more profound when God broke into her silence with a picture of herself as a toddler in a Yugoslavian refugee camp. Though brought up in the USA, Livia was born in Hungary, and in 1956 her parents had to escape from the country. As Livia sat on the sofa, God ministered healing to the tiny Livia who suffered emotional trauma in the harsh conditions of the camp.

Hearing God

As I have already suggested, the more we spend time with God in silent prayer, the more we slow down and, together, they lead to an enhanced sensitivity to his voice. Despite his full days of ministry, I believe Jesus lived with an inner silence and stillness at all times that allowed him to be open to what God was telling him to do. In our busy and fast lives, we often overlook God's voice or leading, which can come in many ways. I will share with you two examples from among many that I've experienced.

God spoke to me so many times when he was leading me to Canada. On one such occasion, I was attending an evangelistic event on a sweltering summer evening in Wales with Morgan, a new friend (from Canada!). The organizers had kindly placed dozens of bottles of water on the tables, though we hadn't paid them any attention. The speaker suddenly spoke a few words that grabbed my attention, as though he had turned the volume up: ". . . and God will make it very clear." At that moment, Morgan nudged me and indicated the water bottle on our table. The label on the bottle read, "Clearly Canadian." We walked around the auditorium at the end and couldn't find another bottle of that brand!

As I already shared, after Regent College I nursed my mother through dementia to her passing and found myself about to be without a home but also in need of a long rest. With only a few weeks before I had to move, I journeyed across England to visit some friends I'd made at Regent College, and we prayed about my situation. The return trip involved three trains and, on each one, I found myself sitting across a table from a German-speaking lady, a different one each time. At home, I pondered on this and decided it was too much of a coincidence. "Father," I prayed, "what are you trying to say?" Immediately the words "Schloss Mittersill" came into my mind. The Schloss was a Christian community and study center in the Austrian Alps with a connection to Regent College. I'd once heard of it but long forgotten about it. I contacted the community and discovered they had a sabbatical program perfect for me. I was on my way within two weeks, an opportunity I could easily have missed.

Humility

My list of the fruits of silent prayer is far from exhaustive. Rather I have written on those things that the Lord brought to my attention. But I can't close this chapter without mentioning humility, a theme that recurs throughout medieval spiritual writings, both as a fruit of contemplative prayer and a prerequisite to further progress. Teresa of Avila suggested that without such humility, we will not make progress in the contemplative life. There is not space here to do the subject justice, but it is worthy of further study.

Chapter 9—Another Way

As I suggested earlier, for those unable to spend extended quality time with God in abiding prayer, there is another way we can give a substantial part of our time to him, even within a busy life. *The Practice of the Presence of God* is a collection of writings by Brother Lawrence, a seventeenth-century French monk that, like Teresa of Avila's *The Interior Castle,* has found its way into the hands of many modern Christians. While the book is attributed to him, it was written after his death by a cleric, Abbé Joseph de Beaufort, from conversations with him about his spiritual life. The abbé, in his short account of the life of Brother Lawrence in some translations of the book, leaves us a picture of Lawrence at work: "Even when he was busiest in the kitchen, it was evident that the brother's spirit was dwelling in God. He often did the work that two usually did, but he was never seen to bustle. Rather, he gave each chore the time that it required, always preserving his modest and tranquil air, working neither slowly nor swiftly, dwelling in calmness of soul and unalterable peace."[1]

As mentioned in the previous chapter, one fruit of silence and contemplative prayer is that, given time, we carry the silence with God out into everyday life, a kind of active contemplation where we continue to be aware of God on the edge of our vision. This happens naturally and without effort, but Brother Lawrence took it a step further. Though his silence in the presence of God may have been initially fashioned through silent prayer, he attempted to focus regularly on God throughout the day, approaching something that Paul might have meant when he exhorted us

---

1. Lawrence, *Practice of Presence*, 83–84.

to "pray continually" (1 Thessalonians 5:17). Of course, the same might be said of active contemplation. Brother Lawrence stated: "If the will can in any fashion understand God, it can only be through love . . . I do nothing else but abide in his holy presence, and I do this by a simple attentiveness and an habitual, loving turning of my eyes on him. This I should call . . . a wordless and secret conversation between the soul and God which no longer ends."[2] Though he had no position or influence, his daily tasks being confined to the monastery kitchen, his character, and the peace surrounding him attracted many to travel to the monastery to seek spiritual guidance from him.

Frank Laubach was a twentieth-century missionary who also wrote on practicing God's presence in two small booklets: *Letters by a Modern Mystic* and *Games with Minutes*. If Brother Lawrence provided the initial theory, then Frank Laubach wrote practically on the "how," suggesting an artificial but effective way to live one's days in God's presence by learning to bring Christ to mind in each minute of the day. As with Brother Lawrence, Laubach's influence was wide-ranging, and he was much loved. Their writings are gathered together in a book called *Practicing His Presence* (The Library of Spiritual Classics), volume 1, a worthwhile read.

Thomas R. Kelly, another missionary and contemporary of Frank Laubach, also wrote on practicing the presence of God in his book, *A Testament of Devotion*. He suggested a dichotomy between two levels of our minds, the upper secular mind and the "deeper level, where the soul ever dwells in the presence of the Holy One."[3] He stated that "at first the practice of inward prayer is a process of alternation of attention between outer things and the Inner Light. Preoccupation with either brings the loss of the other. Yet what is sought is not alternation, but simultaneity, worship undergirding every moment, living prayer, the continuous current and background of all moments of life. Long practice

2. Blaiklock trans., *Practice of Presence*, 73, 44.

3. Kelly, *Testament*, 10.

indeed is needed before alternation yields to concurrent immersion in both levels at once."[4]

When taken together, the writings of these three authors, especially initially Laubach, with his *Game with Minutes*, will provide the theory and practical steps into practicing the presence of God, like silent prayer a spiritual discipline for all believers. Undoubtedly, for Jesus, it was a perfectly natural practice; his focus would have been on the Father all the time, anyway.

As for its fruits, they would be more difficult to define, though similar to those I've mentioned in chapter 8 for silent prayer. But I think they would require far more practice to appear, given the focused time set aside for silent prayer.

4. Kelly, *Testament*, 13.

Chapter 10—My Story

ALTHOUGH WE SHARE A general Christian story, Jesus leads each of us differently, and the particular experiences that God uses to transform us are unique to each person. I decided to share *my* testimony to provide a context for my journey into silence, nothing more. It's not vital that you read this, but it might provide some understanding.

In the early 1990s, when I was in my mid-thirties, my life fell apart on every material level. My former wife left me for a close friend. And a new job turned out to be a terrible mistake, and through it, I lost my home and savings, basically everything. Without a home, I slept on my mother's sofa while I tried to find suitable work, but it was in short supply, and a job recruiter I signed up with had to comb the entire country for me.

My family background was nominally Anglican, which meant attending a service perhaps at Easter and Christmas. In hindsight, I would have to go back to the seventeenth century to find an ancestor who was a "real" Christian. And to be honest, I despised everything about Christianity and God, thinking him cold and distant like the churches I'd encountered.

No one had invited me to church before, so it was a surprise when a neighbor of my mother invited me to a local Pentecostal church, but I slipped through his fingers. A month later, I received another invitation from someone else but to the same church. Coincidence, I wondered? But again, I made excuses. Finally, struggling with my unemployment, I went to see the employer I worked for before my "terrible mistake," to see if she had any work she could send my way. Sadly, no. But before I left, her face lit up, and she said, "Guess what! I've become a Christian, and I go to . . ." Before she could finish, I knew beyond any doubt that she went to the same Pentecostal church and wondered what on earth was going on!

Feeling safer attending with her, I went to see if I could find any answers. You'll perhaps understand that since my only experience of church was the Church of England, I found people in the Pentecostal church to be overwhelmingly friendly but weird, very weird. Tongues! Hands in the air!

But in my vulnerable state, I was thankful for the fellowship on Sunday, even if I couldn't buy into the Gospel message I heard preached each week. On my third Sunday, the pastor announced that a girl would be baptized that evening in the private swimming pool next door . . . and did anyone else want to be baptized? Much to my surprise, my hand went up, and I pulled it down quickly. But the congregation and pastor had seen me, so he spent five minutes trying to persuade me to go ahead as I backpedaled, explaining that I didn't believe in this stuff.

But I finally relented—he would not take no for an answer, and the people were so kind I didn't want to disappoint them—though I recognized it was probably the stupidest thing I'd ever done in my life. As I sat in shock, the pastor explained that I should wear white clothes for the baptism and come with a change of clothes. I foresaw a problem there. I nearly always wear dark clothing, and having stayed away from home the previous night, I'd only packed a few clothes. But when I checked, I had exactly what I needed—I recalled packing a white shirt and trousers because, for some bizarre reason I didn't question, I thought I might need them!

That Sunday evening, I was led into the pool by two hefty elders, who looked as though they'd been chosen to make sure I went through with it, and with the same unspiritual thoughts rattling through my mind. All I can say is that I went under the water an unbelieving cynic and came up Spirit-filled, knowing God as my Father, Jesus Christ as my Savior, and with the voices of a heavenly choir echoing in the roof of the pool. If that wasn't enough, I came to recognize that although I'd grown up frightened of my father, I could approach my heavenly Father without a trace of fear, and from that moment, he has been the member of the Trinity I most readily relate to.

By that time, the job recruiter had found me two potential positions in the UK, and they were both in the same small town in Wales. Both jobs were offered to me, and I recognized that's where God wanted me. The Anglican church there turned out to be so different from anything I'd experienced of that denomination and an ideal place for a new Christian to be.

If there was a blot on this idyllic time, it was my worsening health as the headaches and migraines I'd experienced from time to time grew more intense and frequent. After two years, I was "let go" by my employers because of too many days off. My attendance at church and home groups was also sporadic, though I managed to get through the Alpha course. But life *was* idyllic, spiritually, and I experienced several profound encounters with God. On one occasion, while doing dishes after a home group, I became suddenly filled with an explosive sense of joy that had me dancing around the vicarage kitchen. It turned out that the employer I'd witnessed to had just given his life to the Lord, and I had been invited into the heavenly celebrations. There were many others. I've already mentioned my unwitting witness to women on a train and my encounter with God on a beach when he put his arms around me. He released me after perhaps half a minute, but next to my conversion, those were probably the most significant thirty seconds of my life.

From that moment on, I've unconsciously sought that degree of silent intimacy with God again. He said nothing, but words were unnecessary—and they still are. It's possible, though maybe unlikely, that God will grace me with a similar sense of his presence and love again in this life, but no matter. I felt I was experiencing a small taste of what his love would feel like in heaven, but with the disadvantage of an earthly body ill-equipped to receive it.

Unemployed during a lovely summer, I rested and spent time on the beach, seeking Christian work rather than what I'd been doing. Just as the weather cooled, a brother in Christ offered me a job like my old one. It was not what I wanted, but I felt God saying it would only be for an interim time.

Within a year, God was telling me to travel to Canada and study at Regent College, an evangelical graduate school of theology in Vancouver. I had no aspirations either to leave the UK or to study at a Bible or theological college. But God made his will so ridiculously obvious to me that in October 1996 I went, wondering why he would send me almost halfway around the world when there were excellent colleges available in the UK. The answer became clear when, with advice from Dr. James Houston, I signed up for a master's degree in spiritual theology: the study of prayer and other aspects of the relationship between God and ourselves. In the late 1990s, few if any evangelical seminaries offered a degree in such a subject.

My migraines and headaches became more regular, not helped by the pressures of study, much as I loved it, and I registered as "disabled," which allowed me to finish papers in my own time rather than to the normal deadlines. It was a wonderful time, hugely expanding the horizons of what I understood to be prayer and providing affirmation and a theological framework to my experiences of God so far. It was a time, too, when the God I knew grew infinitely larger and worthy of my trust as my need to analyze and control him diminished. It took me longer to complete the degree than normal, but that proved to be a blessing too. When it came to the final comprehensive paper, a kind of mini-thesis, rather than write on a standard list of spirituality books, God made it clear he wanted me to write on the practice of contemplative prayer. It turned out to be a labor of love.

Returning to the UK hoping to go into ministry, I found my mother in the early stages of dementia, and God told me I would look after her until she died. It was a difficult few years at the end of which I was on the edge of burnout and depression, but in early 2003, he led me to Schloss Mittersill, a Christian community and study center in the Austrian Alps, to rest for a year. Having just lived an isolating existence with no social life, I threw myself into community, but as I recovered, God drew me away into increasing times of silence that became the highlight of my day.

I stayed on to run the library and met my wife, Livia, a missionary working in Hungary. After a few years, it became clear God wanted us in Northern Scotland, where we still live. My health has continued to deteriorate, where daily migraines and severe headaches have made it impossible to engage in any regular work, and I've also struggled with cancer and other debilitating health issues. Despite so much prayer for my healing, I've come to believe God wants me to remain physically weak and dependent on him for everything in my life. I am. I can't take anything for granted. I need his grace and strength to even get up in the morning, let alone get in the car and drive somewhere. I ask him to take these problems from me but then pray for his will to be done, not mine. It doesn't occur to me to be angry with him; he loves me and knows what's best.

Ironically, I feel so blessed. Despite the pain I suffer from much of my waking hours, I know so much peace and quiet strength, emotionally and spiritually. God's overwhelming love for me is my constant companion, and I have no questions regarding my faith, little that I struggle with. In *The Message* translation of Matthew 11:28–30, Jesus said, "Walk with me and work with me—watch how I do it. Learn the unforced rhythms of grace. . . . Keep company with me and you'll learn to live freely and lightly." I can identify with these words. But it is nothing for me to boast about. I'm still on the road, a work in progress, and it is all God's work, anyway. But I can recognize that the many hours I've spent in solitude and silence, just sitting with and abandoned to God, have been fundamental to any progress I might have made. This is not a boast either. Day after day, his direction, grace, and strength have led me into that hour of his loving company.

Conclusion

IN THE BEGINNING, GOD created us for a relationship of love with him, to share in the abundant mutual love of the Trinity. But we are broken people, and receiving that love at more than a superficial theological level is hard unless we make ourselves available to God, unless we spend time with him without filling it with our own voices.

We need to abandon ourselves to him regularly and allow him to love us in the silence. If we don't, then our identity will never be in him, as it should be, but in what we *do* for him, in our ministry, and what we do for the church. And that can inevitably become busy and fraught because guilt and the feeling we're not doing enough never allows us to say no. These are not the "unforced rhythms of grace"[1] that Jesus promised us, not the living "freely and lightly."[2] Add to that, ministry isn't as effective as it should be because desirous of pleasing or appeasing God, we run ahead of him, busy in what we're doing, sure that he'll be pleased with us and bless our efforts. But why should he? Those are our plans, not his.

In contrast, Jesus knew the Father's love and never tried to earn it, but in putting the Father first in the hours he spent with him, Jesus had such a close relationship that he knew what the Father wanted of him at all times, and he only did what he saw the Father doing. Nothing more. Furthermore, he was empowered to do the things God gave him to do. The priority was relationship and should be for us if we want to enjoy the unforced rhythms of grace and a relaxed and simple Christian life.

1. Matthew 11:28–30 (MSG).
2. Matthew 11:28–30 (MSG).

Summing up the Ten Commandments, Jesus told us: "'Love the Lord your God with all your heart and with all your soul and with all your mind.' This is the first and greatest commandment. And the second is like it: 'Love your neighbor as yourself.'"[3]

Note that the first commandment is the greatest. If we and the church would only recognize that and put God first, ahead of any ministry, then things would fall into their rightful place. "Seek first his kingdom and his righteousness, and all these things will be given to you as well" (Matthew 6:33). Again the same message. And in the story of Mary and Martha, it was Mary who was commended for sitting at Jesus' feet, rather than Martha, who was busy ministering to the Lord. The message is clear. Relationship with God is primary, with ministry and mission secondary and flowing out of the relationship. To paraphrase C. S. Lewis, put God first, rather than works for him, then the works will follow almost organically. But putting God first means filling our days with him. Not the things of him but him alone and his presence, abandoned in silence to his love and guidance.

It's so simple and yet so profound.

3. Matthew 22:37–39.

Bibliography

Ashbrook, R. Thomas. *Mansions of the Heart: Exploring the Seven Stages of Spiritual Growth*. San Francisco: Jossey-Bass, 2009. A modern and helpful systematic analysis of Teresa of Avila's book, *The Interior Castle* and guide into her mansions of prayer.

Blaiklock, E. M., trans. *The Practice of the Presence of God*. London: Hodder & Stoughton, 1996.

Hooper, Walter, ed. *The Collected Letters of C.S. Lewis, Vol. III, Narnia, Cambridge and Joy, 1950-1963*. San Francisco: Harper, 2007.

Houston, James M., ed. *A Life of Prayer*. Classics of Faith and Devotion, ed. James M. Houston. Minneapolis: Bethany House, 1998. An annotated selection of the writings of Teresa of Avila, including *The Interior Castle*.

———. *The Transforming Friendship: A Guide to Prayer*. Vancouver, Canada: Regent College, 2010.

Jethani, Skye. *With: Reimagining the Way You Relate to God*. Nashville: Thomas Nelson, 2011. A book that addresses the ways in which our relationship to God is distorted.

Kelly, Thomas R. *A Testament of Devotion*. San Francisco: Harper Collins, 1996. Includes deeper discussion of practicing the presence of God as well as other mystical writings.

Lawrence, Brother. *The Practice of the Presence of God*. New Kensington, PA: Whitaker House, 1982.

Lawrence, Brother, and Frank Laubach. *Practicing His Presence*. Library of Spiritual Classics, Vol. 1, Beaumont: The Seed Sowers, 1973. A volume that includes *The Practice of the Presence of God,* by Brother Lawrence together with the writings of Frank Laubach.

Ryrie, Alexander. *Silent Waiting: The Biblical Roots of Contemplative Spirituality*. Norwich, UK: Canterbury, 1999.

Young, William P. *The Shack*. Los Angeles: Windblown Media, 2007.

Printed in Great Britain
by Amazon

24837160R00040